Nine Lives Nine Purses

Holding down a job while gripping Louie

SHEILA SCHULTZ

©2024 Sheila Schultz. All rights reserved.

No part of this book may be reproduced or transmitted in any form or by any means, electronic or mechanical, including photocopying, recording or by any information storage or retrieval system, except as may be expressly permitted by law or in writing from the publisher, or except by a reviewer who may quote brief passages in review to be printed in a magazine, newspaper, or online website.

Permission should be addressed in writing to remmie560@gmail.com

I have tried to recreate events, locales, and conversations from my memories of them. In order to maintain their anonymity, in some instances, I may have changed the names of individuals and places, some identifying characteristics and details such as physical properties, occupations, and places of residence.

Edited by Philip S Marks

Cover and formatting by Ginger Marks, DocUmeant
https://documeantdesigns.com/

ISBN: 9798877108035

To my sweet little angels, my granddaughters, Adalynn and Everly. I got the best of two worlds with Adalynn being my blonde hair and blue eyed girl (from her grandfather's side) and Everly carrying on the Japanese side, looking so Asian.

Aishitemasu always,

Sheshe

Contents

Acknowledgments ix
Introduction xi
    Thirty Marines xiii

Modeling Career 1
    The Rock 1
    Isty Bitsy Teenie Weenie Bikini 2
    No Hurrying Traditions 3
    Two Sumos And The Wrestler 3
    Texas 4
    Am I A Lesbian? 4
    Who Nose a Cowboy? 5
    Commodore 64 5
    Lie Detector? 6
    21st Century Jobs 6
    Waterless Pool? 7
    Don't Judge Me 7
    Cake Anyone? 8
    The Covered Bridge 9
    Humble Pie 9

Paris 10
    Disney Princess? 11

Ten Years Later 12
    The Louie Vuitton Experience 13

    A World Of Intrigue 14

    Introducing, Miss Tilla. 15

    I Had My Guard Up. 16

    Capucine. 18

    Damn her To Hell!. 19

    Telling The Truth Is Overrated! 20

    Buyer's Remorse? 20

    The Next Day 21

South of France 22
    Princess of Wales. 22

    Looney Tunes 22

    Off Track. 23

    Avignon. 23

Suffocating Louie 24
    Unsecured 25

Nice, France 26
    Keeping my luggage on a diet the Jenny Craig Way! 27
    MacGyver 29

Italy 31
    Florence and The Hand Molester 31
    Innocence Lost. 33
    Wine Window 35
    Flintstones. 36

Rome 37
    Dead Popes 38
    Cheese Wheel 38
    Three Coin Toss 39
    Lock and Key 39
    Naples. 40
    Best Pizza Ever! 41
    Pizza School. 43
    Disappointment 43
    Venice. 45
    Tom Cruise 45
    Miami Or Bust! 46
    Gondola. 47

England 49

Ladies And Gentlemen, The Beatles. 50

Road Rage? 51

London 52

McDonald's 53

Harrods 53

First Class! 55

Dreading Customs 56

Beat The System 56

Kiss And Tell 57

It's A Wonderful Life 57

Home Sweet Home!. 58

Back To The Grind 59

Goodbye Is Hard 59

The Final Curtain 59

Stone Pizza Oven. 60

About the Author 63

Acknowledgments

TO MY HUSBAND, Jan, my mom, Keiko, my son, Justin, my daughter, Brookelynn, Jessica, and Adalynn, Everly, Tonia, Shane, McKinley, Reese, Maria, Tilla, Phil, Lynn, Brian, Kathy, Tom, Mike, Joyce, Crystal, Tammy, Lizeth, Nina, Denise, and all the customers at the Covered Bridge, as well as all the pets (alive and dead) I've watched , you are (were) all very special to me.

STURGIS
CONCORD
THE CONVENTION CONNECTION
TRADESHOWS & SPECIALIZED SERVICES

Introduction

I was inspired to write this 'coffee-table' type of book after watching Kramer do so on an episode of *Seinfeld*! (I believe Kramer and I have a lot of similarities) I wanted to share with my family and friends some unbelievable adventures from my career and my once-in-a-lifetime trip to Europe and the luxury designer purses that came home with me.

My name is Sheila Monje' Schultz; I am of Japanese and French descent, I embrace my heritage equally, but I have a passion for living life to its fullest and not being afraid to take chances!

Save the date, engagement picture.

Nine Lives—Nine Purses

Sturgis or Bust

I have many hobbies, but I enjoy jumping on my Harley and riding for miles with my husband, Jan. He introduced me to the sport and really expected me to only be a passenger on his bike. When he told me to hop on the back of his motorcycle with a seat that is stuck on by the lick of a rubber suction cup and placed on the fender of his bike! Remember that a motorcycle doesn't have a seat belt so, the only thing that holds you onto the motorcycle is to grip on to the driver's waist with a wish and a prayer! (The seat reminded me of a woman's maxi pad) That's when I told him I would be riding my own motorcycle! I had never ridden a bike in my whole life, but it was time to starting learning and become a 'biker chick'! Jan knew his job of teaching me would be a real test! Between him teaching me to be a safe rider and taking the motorcycle class, I knew I wouldn't be the daredevil desperado that I usually am! Jan had me practice in a large parking lot by our house for THREE months before he believed I was ready to ride on the highway. I thought that those months were a bit of overkill and extremely boring, but I did learn a lot about riding! Almost falling under an oak tree due to wet peat moss (slippery surface) is when I laid the bike down. I tried picking it up by myself and failed miserably. That's when I became so frustrated that I screamed, "I am done!" Jan's encouragement made me realize that I had to, "Get back on the horse," as the saying goes. I did and those three months of boredom made these long rides one of my favorite hobbies. My advice to anyone who wants to ride a motorcycle is to take a course, learn the proper ways of riding, have respect for the motorcycle, be a defensive rider and wear a helmet!

I've had a few jobs in my life. No, if I'm going to be truthful; I've had hundreds of jobs in my lifetime!

Thirty Marines

"I am a Certified Lifeguard." Well, that is what I wanted to become. In reality, what I ended up becoming is a Water, Safety, Survival, Instructor or a WSSI! That was the only course offered to non-military dependents on the base at Okinawa, Japan to become a lifeguard. I had no other choice but to take the class with thirty Marines! The Gunnery Sergeant didn't treat me any differently than the Marines. I went through the training using their military uniform as a floatation device, with a fake gun over my shoulder, learning how to survive treading water in the middle of the Pacific Ocean, for over three hours, in order to pass the course. I chanted

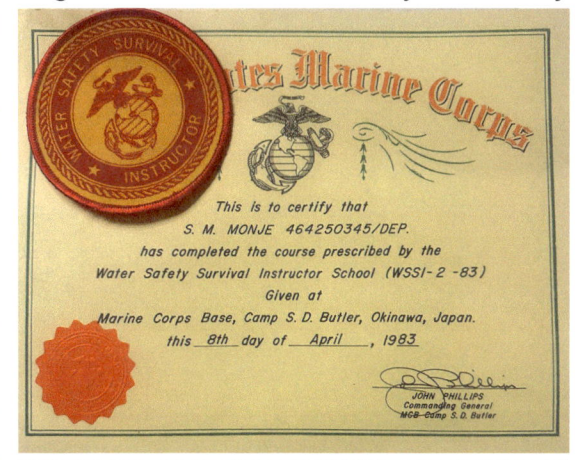

WSSI Certificate

to myself that it would be worth it in the end. Looking back, I think that the Gunnery Sergeant was harder on me because I was the only woman in the class!

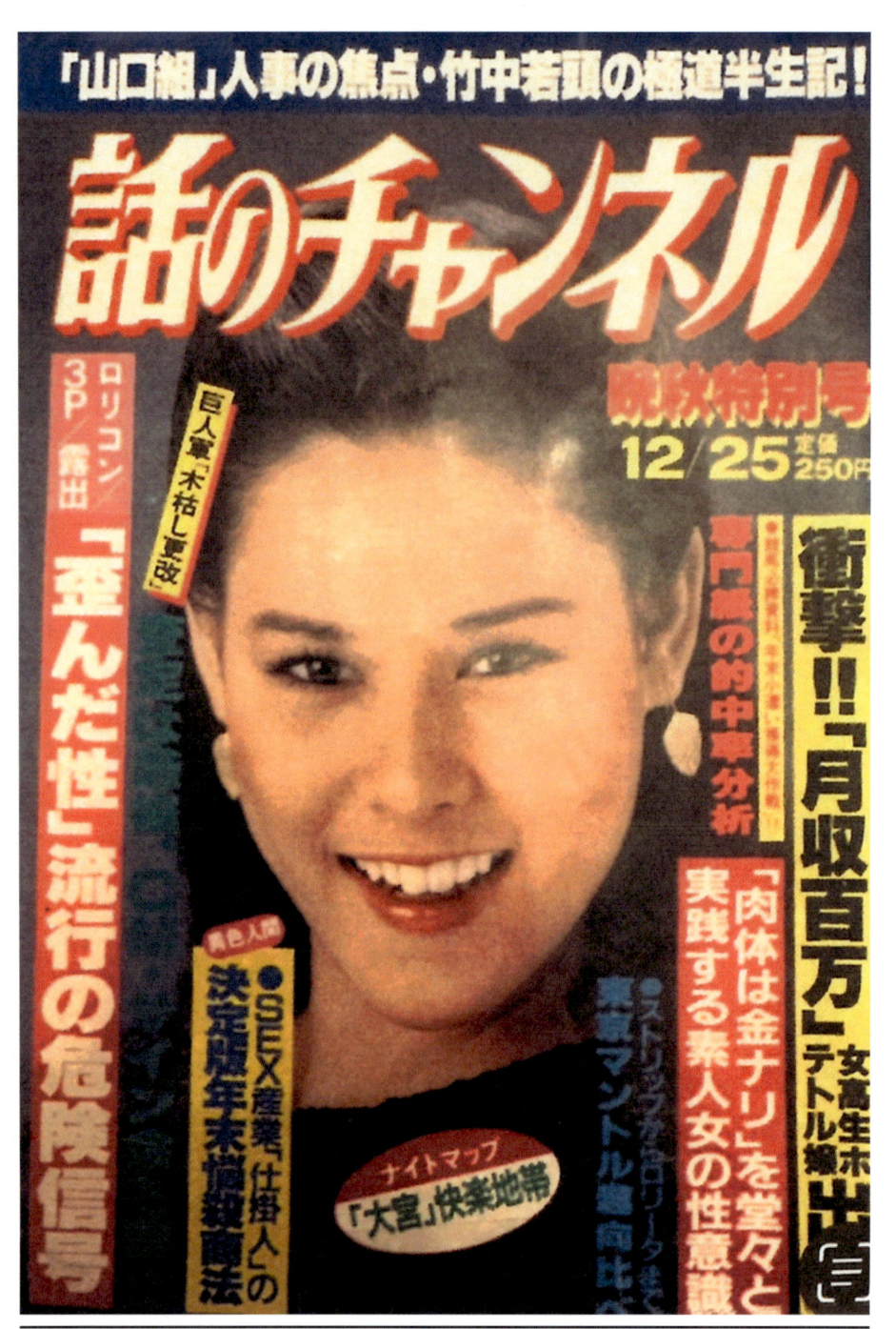

Japanese Playboy

Modeling Career

The Rock

Music cassette mix cover model

While working at a Shakey's Pizza Parlor, on the island of Okinawa a.k.a. The Rock, I was "discovered". I was a model – in Tokyo, Japan! At that time, I was attending Kubasaki High School. I thought it would be easier if I dropped out because I felt I would never have an opportunity like that to model again. With the encouragement of my music teacher, Mr. Hall, who said if the agency really wanted me, they would wait, I decided that school was more important. Mr. Hall was right! The modeling agency flew me back and forth during my last year of school from Okinawa to Tokyo until I graduated and moved to Tokyo. I am so grateful that I didn't quit school!

The agency's name was Olive Modeling Company. Right away the agency tried to train me to be an obedient little Japanese girl with all the traditional customs; like walking ten paces behind a man, bowing and saying a Japanese phrase; *Douzo yoroshiku onegaishimasu* which translates to, it's so nice to meet you. It wasn't a very easy task because of my Texas accent!

Isty Bitsy Teenie Weenie Bikini

It was time for me to show my worth with the modeling agency. I made it onto a Japanese show called, "The 11 PM Show". When I was interviewing for the show, I was taken to a building full of only Japanese women. It reminded me of cattle, that's probably why they call it a "cattle call".

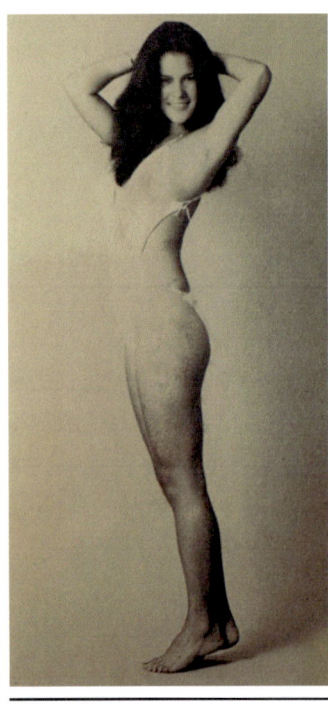

Test shot

I was the only American there and it was very intimidating to say the least. I had asked the Scout (a person that takes you for interviews) why I was there. With tears streaming down my face, I told my Scout that I wanted to leave. He told me not to cry. He told me that he had a secret weapon for me. I asked him what it was, and he reached into his pocket and pulled out the tiniest bikini and told me that if I wore it, I would for sure get the job. When I went to the interview, there were ten Japanese businessmen asking me all sorts of questions in Japanese. Smiling and looking lost was all I could do because I didn't know the language.

A week later, I got a call at my agency that I had gotten the job! This show introduces you as a new up-and-coming model. I rode a bullet train from Tokyo to Kyoto where the show aired. When

I went up to the penthouse, waiting for me was a big basket of fruit and champagne. It made me feel like royalty.

Everything was running smoothly; until it was time for me to change into a bikini. I had taken off my belt that was wrapped around my waist, (the style in the 80s)only to have red marks from the impression of the belt. The staff were all panicked because I was supposed to go on air within the hour! They talked about putting body makeup on me, I told them if they left it alone the marks would disappear! Sure enough, the marks went away.

No Hurrying Traditions

The Japanese bow when they meet and part from one another (Westerners use a handshake) to express gratitude, to show deference to superiors, and in many other social situations. I sat on a city bus and watched as two little old Japanese women bowed to each other numerous times. The bus driver didn't move an inch or say a word as to hurry the ladies along. When the women were finished bowing to one another and entered the bus, the bus driver resumed his route.

Two Sumos And The Wrestler

One of my many experiences, while modeling and living in Tokyo, was when I ran into Terry Funk, a professional wrestler, who started his wrestling career in 1965 in Amarillo, Texas.

By the 80s, his career started slowing down in the states, so he relocated to Tokyo to wrestle. (Which by the way, the Japanese adored him.) I just happened to be in an elevator when Terry and two Sumos entered. You could tell that the Sumos were disinterested in being with him, but it was their job to be his body guards! He looked over at me and started saying some inappropriate things. I assumed he didn't think I could speak English. I let it go on for a while until I had enough. I stopped him from making a big fool of himself and said, "You know Terry, the guys in Texas would kick your ass for what you're saying to a lady." We both had a laugh about it and the next thing I knew I was dancing at the club between two Sumos! (They bounced me around like a rag doll!)

When my son, Justin was young he really loved to watch wrestling and he came out of his room and called me a S.O.B. from what he learned on the television. I asked him where he heard that phrase from and he said, "It was from a guy named Terry Funk, the wrestler!"

How could I be mad?! (I recently learned that Terry Funk went to wrestling heaven in August of 2023.)

Texas

After high school, I returned stateside and ended up moving to Texas on an airline called, "The Flying Tigers". It was a military airline that could fly over three hundred military guys at a time. There were only four females on the flight including myself!

Texas was where I was raised . I had two brothers who lived there along with my first love, Rodney. At the time, Rodney was the reason for my return to the states. That turned out to be a disappointment, but I had to find out for myself if there was a future with him. That was the main reason I left my modeling career behind.

The only thing I found was that I was lonely, broke, and needed a job!

Am I A Lesbian?

Having no college or trade, I interviewed to be a cocktail waitress at a bar called Stanleys. They staffed gay people but catered to straight clientele. I knew my interview had to credible because I was being interviewed by a woman named Melons. I desperately needed the job, so I pretended I was a lesbian.

Who Nose a Cowboy?

I quickly learned that in Texas they don't mess around when they say that drinks need to be off the tables at a certain time. If the authorities find a drink on the table one minute later, they will pull the liquor license and fine the establishment heavily. One example is when Frenchy, the bartender, told a cowboy and his two girlfriends that at 1:45 a.m., he would be collecting their drinks. The next thing I knew the two were fighting and Frenchy got up spitting. I found it strange but thought it was how a cowboy ends a fight.

Frenchy approached me with his hand in his pocket asking if I wanted to see something! The curiosity got the best of me, and I replied, "Yes, what is it?" It was the cowboy's nose! Frenchy had bitten the tip completely off! I quit that night!

Commodore 64

The next day, I applied for a job at a computer store that sold Commodore 64s. I knew absolutely nothing about computers, but I did know how to talk. I interviewed and was honest, telling the owner, John, that I didn't even know how to turn the computer on. It didn't seem to faze him at all, John told me I got the job because I spelled computers right!

All they wanted me for was to be another Vanna White like the television show "Wheel of Fortune".

I got people to talk to the four-hundred-pound smart geek, that would hide in the back. The geek was scary to look at but knew his computer stuff!

Lie Detector?

Next, I went for an interview at a lumberyard. The manager was looking forward to me working there. So much so, he prematurely put me on the schedule and told me the only thing I needed to do beforehand was to go down and take a lie detector test; a requirement to work there. I've never taken one before, so I was very nervous. The guy that was conducting the lie detector machine told me to just relax and be truthful! The first question was, while employed, had I taken anything that wasn't mine?

I couldn't stop thinking about when I was a child and stole a candy bar from a candy store. Another time was when I worked at a bakery, and they told me to throw all the pastries away at the end of the day. I was like Lucy from the "I Love Lucy" show when she kept eating all the candy off of the conveyor belt as they were falling off! Needless to say, I failed the lie detector test and was taken off the schedule!

The next job I had was at a bank and I didn't have to take a lie detector test to work there!

Nothing ever seems to make sense to me. I couldn't be trusted with a piece of plywood, but I could be trusted with handling millions of dollars of businesses and people's money!

21st Century Jobs

I owned a cleaning service with a contract with a major electric company as one of my clients. I have monitored swimming pools, adding chemicals to them when necessary, ran a pet sitting service, and fed the hungry.

At this time in my life, I had been employed for over forty-four years and you would think with age would come wisdom. However, the failed jobs still continue to haunt me. No job ever ran entirely smoothly. The following are a few examples.

Waterless Pool?

I took care of a friend's pool for three months. Everything was going great until the day I went to pour the chemicals into the water only to discover an empty pool! Where did the water go?! A $5.00 part broke and drained the pool of all of its water. We remained friends to this day—they actually wanted me to watch their pool again!

Don't Judge Me

Please hear me out before you judge me. I've had animals die in my care!

For over ten years, I was employed by a married couple to care for their five dogs when the couple went out of town. (Fun fact the lady's father invented the laser pointer.) Obviously, as time passed the dogs aged. Unbeknown to me, the Veterinarian had informed the couple that two of their pets were on borrowed time.

I watched the dogs on Friday, and all was well. Saturday morning, Shadie laid down and never got up again. I was truly a wreck and called my husband, Jan, who immediately came over to help me.

When I called the couple to inform them of the sad event, they told me to deal with it! I was instructed to place Shadie in a plastic container and take her to their vet to hold 'til their return the following Saturday. I neglected to mention that the couple were hoarders. So, finding a container was no easy task—nor was placing Shadie in the container.

I believe that they knew what was going to occur and that's why the couple had left town. After taking care of Shadie, I looked over at Powder, the other dog, and realized that he too was on his last leg. I begged him not to die, especially on my watch. The owners returned on Saturday, as promised, and Powder went to doggie heaven on Sunday.

When covid ended, the couple begged me to watch their remaining three dogs so they could travel again. They tried to entice me by taking me out to dinner but at that point I knew that I couldn't go through all the grief again. I finally mustered up the courage to tell them I had *enough*!

This picture is one of my husband's favorite pictures of me with the Tampa Bay Buccaneer Cheerleaders. I was asked by the captain of the Buccaneer's ship to be in the Gasparilla parade!

Cake Anyone?

Another time, I was employed to watch a woman's cats that had been rescued from a shelter. One cat was 17 and the other was 18 years old; they did not look too healthy. You guessed it! One of the cats died on my watch! I immediately called Jan who responded, "Not another one!"

I have over 30 years on these gals.

It was time to inform the owner and, of course, she couldn't return until the following day. So, I asked her what I should do with the cat. She instructed me to place it in the freezer. I wrapped the cat in a blanket, opened the freezer and there sat a big birthday cake. I had no choice but to place her cat on top of the cake! You can't make this stuff up!

The Covered Bridge

I've worked at The Covered Bridge for eight years now with a great bunch of people, we are family. It is, by far, the best job that I have ever had. It's a place for me to escape my concerns and get paid well. The owners are not typical bosses, they are friends who care for their employees and customers. They'll do anything for a person—even if it costs them to do it.

One example was when my mother passed away during Hurricane Irma in 2017. The restaurant had to evacuate for that whole week. The approval to reopen was given for the same day as my mom's service. The Covered Bridge didn't hesitate to stay closed out of respect for the loss of my mother. Everyone attended with no thought about the money that could have been made.

I will always remember their kindness. I don't believe that any other company would have cared that much. I really am appreciative and grateful for having these wonderful people in my life.

Humble Pie

I've done it all, I've worked hard all my life and tried never to take shortcuts. I believe that has made me a very humble person. Like everyone else, I've had happy times and sad times. Reflecting on everything, it all comes down to what makes us get up in the mornings, look at ourselves, and love the person in the mirror—even if it takes a little plastic surgery! *wink*

I took my mother's passing hard, but as I glimpse the reflection in the mirror, I see her staring back at me. So, I haven't really lost her completely.

Aishitemasu Okasan! (I love you mama, in Japanese)

Paris

Paris is the city that ignites my imagination and my soul! Maybe it was just in my head how wonderful the city is; it wasn't the people that fascinated me but the beauty of the city that I could paint as a mural on my walls at home – my interpretation of what Paris looked like and felt like until the day that I could actually travel to and experience Paris for myself!

I have to mention that it was Jan, my husband, who fulfilled those dreams for me. When Jan proposed, he asked where I would like to go for our honeymoon; he didn't have to ask me twice to either question! So, in 2023, on my 50th birthday Jan made my dreams come true!

(I planned the anniversary and birthday dates so close together that he wouldn't

Holding Down a Job While Gripping Louie

forget either in the future. Also, I had forewarned him to never combine the two gifts!) We went to Paris without a plan, deciding it was more adventurous to just wander around and explore. It was the trip of a lifetime and as wonderful as I had imagined!

My Prince charming

Not one designer bag came home with me on that trip!

Disney Princess?

We made our way to Disneyland in Paris, France as a wedding gift from my very old friend, Larry! The ironic thing about going to Disney in Paris, is there's a Disney World in Florida that Jan and I have never been to together.

Paris is like Disney World is for so many people, my place to escape to (if only for a short time) and live my dreams. Maybe, I am a Disney princess after all?!

My vision of Paris

11

Ten Years Later

Champagne toast

At this point in my life, I got the job scene down to a science. Now, it was time for me to shop for some luxury items. Even going to Europe wasn't going to be an easy task for me.

In 2023, Jan and I celebrated ten years of marriage by returning to my city—Paris! This time we had an entourage'! Jan's daughter, Tonia, who is a schoolteacher, her husband, Shane a.k.a. MacGyver, and their daughters, McKinley and Reese. McKinley is 20 years old and is celebrating graduating with a Masters Degree! Reese is sixteen and always says, "Oh sugar cookies!" when expressing her anger!

Our trip begins by landing in my city, Paris. This trip I am bringing my love for Louie Vuitton (LV) to fruition; I am choosing a purse (or two or three) to keep reminiscences of Paris with me always! They serve as a constant reminder of all the happy memories, just like a good friend would. It's like a little talisman that keeps me connected to the past. It makes me feel like I'm always carrying a piece of my past with me wherever I go.

Of course, this being the beginning of our trip, I will be carrying LV with me for three and a half weeks! Would it be worth the frustrations you may ask. My response is a resounding, "Hell Yes!" Hold on Louie Vuitton, "I'm on my way!"

The Louie Vuitton Experience

We were barely off the plane when we all made a beeline for the Louie Vuitton store. Instantly, I knew it would be a magical experience for all of us!

Arriving at the store, Jan and Shane immediately scouted out a place where they could sit comfortably because they knew they were going to be there for a very long time. The staff was well aware that men can become very fidgety, so they immediately put some free espressos in front of them and enticed them with champagne that would follow.

I glanced over at our guys and watched out of the corner of my eye, Shane lifting up his tiny cup with his pinky finger properly extended high in the air, sipping his coffee, and reviewing the room. I am sure he was thinking that everything in the store was overpriced! Jan sipped his expresso thinking to himself *this coffee is in the tiniest cup ever, why wouldn't they put them in a big gulp cup size instead*? As time passed, I did see Jan turn a little pale. Was it because he had one too many expressos or was it because they kept bringing more purses out, and wondering how in the world would he pay for all that I picked out?

We girls were in heaven; looking, dreaming, and choosing the purses that we wanted; similar to the children in the *Willy Wonka and the Chocolate Factory* movie picking all the candy that they could see!

The purses that we chose would only be placed on our shelves like trophies to admire and only be used on special occasions. They may not be made of gold, but we would treat them that way!

A World Of Intrigue

Channel, LV, Gucci, Dior, and Hermes are just a few luxury designers that sell in stores, boutiques, and online. There are consignment stores online such as Fashionfile, The RealReal, Poshmark, and eBay that cater to people that want to sell their used designer purses and also, buy pre-loved luxury designer purses. There's even a guide that will tell you the different degrees of wear which determines the worth of it! Don't be misguided into believing you will get a deep discount because some of these purses can sell for over fifty thousand dollars on up, even secondhand!

There's actually a designer called Hermes that sells to who they want to! With Hermes, you must first build a relationship with the sales associate, they might call you and suggest something that they want you to buy even if you aren't interested in it.

Spending thousands of dollars on accessories, which they expect you to do, doesn't always guarantee you a purse from them!

Saying "NO", when a Hermes sales associate calls to anything they suggest could bump you from getting a purse in the future! You can't just walk into their store uninvited and pick out a luxury purse no matter how much money you put in front of them. There are people that will teach you what you should or should never do in the Hermes Boutiques!

In most luxury designer purse stores, there is always a line outside of people waiting to get inside, some get lucky and get in without an appointment! NEVER expect to get any type of discount on anything in the store no matter how loyal of a customer you are. "DISCOUNT" isn't in their vocabulary. Crazy world of Luxury purses, I know!

Introducing, Miss Tilla

Introducing Miss Tilla

Miss Tilla is the reason that I chose the purses that I did and why the Louie Vuitton shopping experience was a wonderful one-of-a-kind adventure. I was expecting that we would be rushed around the store by a snobbish French sales clerk. I had experienced so much anxiety prior to arrival that I had researched the purses that I planned to purchase, so I would not take too much of the sales clerk's time. Surprisingly, we had the best Sales Associate!

Tilla is a striking beauty with blonde hair, blue eyes, legs up to her neck and a sweet, innocent smile!

I Had My Guard Up

In a boxing match, protecting oneself is crucial to avoid injury. The two phrases that come to mind are "stay on your toes" to avoid getting hit and "no hitting below the belt" to avoid disqualification.

Using this form of protecting myself I had to do some quick studies on boxing—like Muhammad Ali training for a match. All because of Miss Tilla's intimidation!

Miss Tilla started out acting nonchalant, but I knew her game. She didn't take the approach of being overly aggressive. (A great tactic when first meeting a customer.) Miss Tilla asked if we wanted the grand tour. She wanted us to go upstairs to have champagne and look at the exquisite decoration of the building.

Nothing but the best while we visited Paris, so why not go to The Louie Vuitton Champs-Elysees store which is the company's flagship. The over-the-top beauty of the seven-story rain spears that hung so massively from the top of the ceiling was

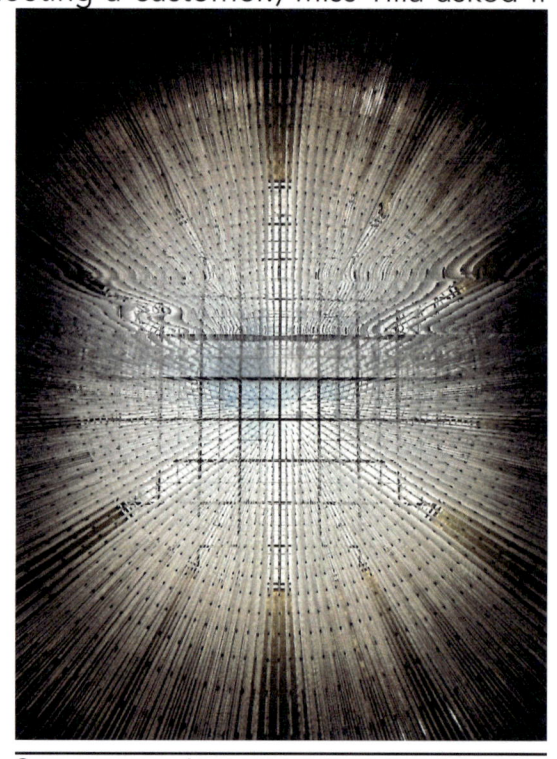

Seven story rain spears

Holding Down a Job While Gripping Louie

breathtaking! We took a picture of it from underneath, and it did look like it was actually raining in the store.

Enough small talk, it was time for us to get down to business. It was like two people sword-fighting, while circling around each other tapping our swords together until someone takes the first plunge. Tilla knew her years of training were about to be put to the test. She turned to me and asked what purses I was interested in.

Immediately I went on the defense! Why would she say plural purses instead of a singular purse? I knew I wanted more than one, but how presumptuous of her!

What a loaded question! With so many to choose from, how in the world could she expect me to narrow it down? I had done my due diligence, and spent many hours of research beforehand, watching endless YouTube luxury purse influencers that I studied morning, noon, and night. I knew I was ready and showed her the pictures of the ones I wanted. She smiled cutely and whispered that I had come prepared.

I had tunnel vision of the only purses I was interested in. There was no way anyone would be able to penetrate my brain and convince me to change what I had already decided upon. It was a done deal; my decision was final. No one could be tricky and talk me into something I didn't want. I wouldn't let it happen, not on my watch! Yes, I was there to buy purses, but I also had to protect my bank account.

I had a price that I wasn't willing to exceed, but Tilla's job was just beginning. This definitely wasn't her first rodeo. She was like a cowboy in the ring, grabbing the bull by the horns, knocking them down to the ground, and roping them off in seconds!

Tilla used the three elements of persuasion on me without my knowledge: logic, ethics, and emotion. Oh, she was so good, she knew exactly what she was doing. It was like the Louie Vuitton store management knew exactly when I walked through the front door and the security parted a pathway that led me to Miss Tilla, like Moses parting the sea. She was the best, and they knew it, and so they teamed me up with her. She was their rock star sales associate.

Miss Tilla's approach was slow and methodical. She knew that deliberately starting with the small stuff of what I thought I wanted would only hold my interest temporarily until the grand finale of what was to come.

Then it happened, it was like a scene from *The Exorcist* where Linda Blair's head does a 180-degree turn. Tilla got into my head, exploited my vulnerability, and had me doing the exact opposite of what I intended.

Capucine

Suddenly, I stopped . . . (dramatic pause)

I told her to please stop, take it away! I had a love/hate relationship with that particular purse. The one purse that I would consider the upper echelon, the one ranked above the others according to its status. The hierarchy of all Louie Vuittons! The purse I would send pictures of to Mckinley and tell her every other day that I was getting, then I would retract what I said.

Miss Capucine

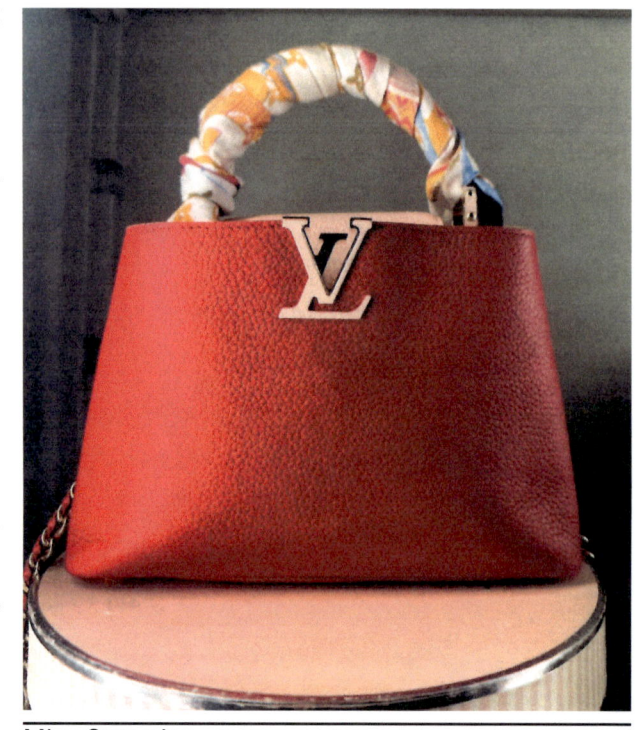

I specifically told Mckinley, under no circumstances to let me get it. I had to restrain myself from the emotion of what I wanted.

There she was, the Capucine . . . when I laid eyes on her, it was like she was taunting me. The feeling was like a baby crying for its mommy and you just have to go pick her up because it's just the right thing to do.

The luxury Capucine purse was then placed in my arms, just like a new born baby. She even had a receiving blanket, which is known as the embroidered dust pounce. Miss Tilla had exposed me to the one purse I told myself I wasn't going to get no matter what.

Damn her To Hell!

I was so enamored by the Capucine purse that immediately I knew she would be coming home with me. In all her two-tone glory, she sported light pink on top with her flair of a darker pink on her bottom. I had made my other choices after about three hours of being there.

Tilla had asked us if we wanted all of our Louie Vuittons delivered to the concierge of our hotel. Wow, that's definitely a first! It was like the feeling in the movie *Titanic* with the ironic railing scene of Jack and Rose and her eyes were closed, it was that intense!

I was then guided to the cashier. Tilla was right by my side making small talk. Of course, she wanted to know what occupation I had. For a brief moment I hesitated, would I be truthful with my answer? Or should I tell her what I wished I were? I began by telling her the truth, that I was a breakfast server and ever since covid I got back into cleaning houses again.

The cleaning jobs had become so profitable for me that I bought myself a new car. I didn't have the guts to tell her that I actually pop out of my new car with a toilet brush in one hand and a bucket in the other ready to clean these houses, especially when

Nine Lives—Nine Purses

I drive up in my Porsche! When I dared to look at Tilla's expression it was like looking at a person in disbelief.

Telling The Truth Is Overrated!

So, I should have just lied and said, "I won the lotto."

You might ask yourself, "is it all worth it?" Cleaning houses, doing odd jobs like landscaping for Mr. Goulash (my nickname for my 92-year-old man because he always wants me to cook Goulash) in 90-degree heat, pet sitting for Izzy, Bumper, and Lucy, working at the Covered Bridge as a server and a cook (especially since I can't cook!) Maybe for some, it's ridiculous, but we all have our own limits and expectations of what we are willing to spend or even how hard we are willing to work. Some feel they have to have material objects, while others would rather take a European vacation and create a memory instead.

Buyer's Remorse?

The LV scarf

I tossed and turned that whole night thinking, was it a little buyer's remorse or why did my new Capucine seem unfinished. There was something missing. Then it happened! I figured it out! Her handle needed to be dressed! She was missing her scarf to cover some of her flashy studs around the jewels that held her together and also to make sure the one person who held her all the time, which would be me, wouldn't get unwanted oils on her from handling her so much. The realization was like an epiphany. I had to buy Capucine a whole wardrobe to complete her!

The Next Day

It was the next morning, and I knew I had to act. So, I marched back to the LV store. If I'm being honest, it was to shop again and to ask Tilla why she didn't suggest the scarf. She said she did, but she could tell I wasn't really into it by my expression.

Of course, she was right, I thought it was an old lady look she gave me, but I can be persuaded! Tilla took time out and showed us exactly how to wrap the scarf around the handle and the many other things the scarf could be used for. It all might be trending now, but it's something that sells at that moment.

I had always loved Paris but now I knew that I had fallen in love with Paris. It truly is one of the best feelings of shopping and was the highlight of our trip!

I guess, if I were asked to compare it to something, it would be like getting a delicious meal when you're on a diet. From the appetizer to the entrée to licking the plate of the dessert. Or when you're in Italy eating the best pizzas ever and you're telling yourself you will only eat two slices and end up eating the whole pizza instead!

South of France

Princess of Wales

As we passed a memorial of Princess Diana and saw where her life was taken too soon, it brought me a little sadness because I really loved her and everything she did for people and the world.

Looney Tunes

While we were heading to the south of France a song infiltrated my conscious. For many years, as a young girl, I could be heard singing one

Princess of Wales Memorial

particular song, and it stuck in my head to this day. So of course, I had to investigate why for years I knew the words but didn't understand what the meaning was.

The song was introduced to the collective consciousness of the American public over a century ago by Sol Bloom, a show business promoter who later became a U.S. Congressman. Bloom was the entertainment director and had written it to build up the 1894 World's Fair.

I can tell you right now that you have to take pretty much any World's Fair story with a grain of salt. There are so many different versions as to how it was created and the different lyrics that I'm just going to go with the following one.

The lyrics go . . . *"There's a place in France where the ladies wear no pants, and the men walk around with their ding dongs hanging down!"*

As Paul Harvey would say, "Now, you know the rest of the story!"

Off Track

Another little tidbit, a lot of areas in France have a pee-pee smell! The French men have a bad B-O while most of the women go around braless. We found out that since 2020 the women have been protesting by not wearing bras! (Luckily, mine are manmade, so I don't have to worry about them hanging low and wobbling to and fro. I'll be letting my boobies hang free.)

Avignon

Continuing on . . . . we arrived in Avignon at a castle and its amazing huge walls that surround the whole village. A festival was going on with street performers. It would have two million people go through it just in the month of July!

Suffocating Louie

Our trip, so far, had been running smoothly until we ran into somewhat of a snag with Sheila doing something really dumb! I put some of my LVs in the hotel safe without reading exactly how to set it. (I followed the pictures displayed but never read the instructions.)

When I went to get them out, the safe wouldn't open. My babies were stuck, suffocating behind the steel! What was I to do but get Shane to the rescue. Shane said it was low on the battery and we needed to locate a 9v battery, of course I wasn't going to admit to doing anything wrong! Where would we get a 9v battery at 11 p.m. in an enclosed castle!?

The guy at the front desk of the hotel was useless and didn't help us. We knew there had to be a master key.

We went from store to store trying to find one; all the stores were closed, of course. While walking, Tonia suggested that maybe the police had 9V in their flashlight, thank god we had enough common sense not to ask to borrow it.

We finally found a French man named, "Francois!" (not kidding) He was very helpful in finding the 9v, but when we tried it; it was unsuccessful. We decided to try and get a locksmith. Francois was kind enough to phone ten different locksmiths with no success. We knew we had to hit the streets of France, once again, in hopes of finding a stronger 9v so Shane could pull off a MacGyver.

Upon our return, all of a sudden, the front desk clerk found a master key and said, "I don't know for sure if this will work." It's a miracle that he pulled it out of his ass! Within seconds the safe opened, it was as simple as simple can be. This definitely called for drinks all around.

Unsecured

After all the security that I thought we were doing to protect my Louies, Jan and I fell asleep from exhaustion with our hotel door unlocked and Louie Vuittons were left out in the open!

Nice, France

We jumped on an express train the following morning. The train goes over 186 miles an hour! Now we were in Nice. First, we went to a flea market that was only open on Mondays. That's where Shane got a really neat old 1930s phone and I picked up a dancing French girl in a bottle. I purchased the bottle with a dancing French girl to remind me of my trip to France which goes along perfectly with my Japanese girl in a bottle that I got as a gift after my mother died.

Ironically it plays one of my mother's favorite songs plus being half-Japanese and half-French, these were meant for me!

Across from our hotel, which overlooked the French Riveria and the Mediterranean Sea, we found ourselves discussing how much we appreciated the soft white sands of Clearwater Beach because it's extremely hard to walk on the pebbles that they have there. While trying to swim in the ocean, Mckinley, Reese, and Shane sacrificed their feet to enjoy the swim. We had a private tour guide who really went above and beyond taking us to the coolest places. We went to Monte Carlo along the French

Riveria known for the world-famous Place du Casino, the gambling center where a James Bond movie was made and also made Monte Carlo an international byword for the extravagant display of the reckless dispersal of wealth. Let's not forget the Monaco Grand Prix!

Keeping my luggage on a diet the Jenny Craig Way!

Let's talk about the failed luggage. Remember, the whole trip was to keep moving around with the least amount of luggage, kind of like backpacking across Europe. Our intention was to exit the plane and be on our way, since we were riding on trains, planes, Ubers, and boats all the time. We started out with a limit, one rolling luggage of 22 lbs. (which is the max for the carry-on for the plane) and one bag to be placed under the seat.

Four days into our trip there was already a major problem with our luggage keeping its girlish figure. It looked like it had hit the buffet line way too many times. It was busting out at the seams. It was definitely at its capacity. So of course, Tonia and I had to go shopping for jumbo-size luggage which we were only too glad to do. We ended up getting a pink one and a blue one. They were so pretty, almost twins!

Trying to get everyone's luggage on and off the trains was a nightmare. The two big jumbos were

The Jenny Craig Way!

shoved under our feet and people were bumping into them. We were given dirty looks by passengers trying to get to their seats.

We were all frustrated with the luggage situation, but I know Tonia and I just didn't want to admit it. Remember we are both strong women and would never admit to being wrong, especially with the luggage . . . until the wheel broke! I had a knot in the bottom of my stomach. *Could it be fixed*? Luckily the screws just fell out and it could be repaired with a screwdriver, not a butter knife, so now we had to look for a screwdriver!

Jan made the decision for me and said it wasn't worth lugging all the luggage around from place to place. So, I caved. Jan was right. He was convinced I would be eliminating the larger blue luggage. All I can say is, "Fat chance!" (Even if it was under my breath so that he didn't hear.)

It ended up costing a whopping $250 to send the treasures we bought home. We used FedEx to ship them. Was it worth it? Well, of course, Jenny Craig would be so proud of us! An instant weight loss, I lost 50 lbs. in 15 minutes. Now, I could do more shopping without worry!

Tonia and Shane decided they would tough it out with their pink luggage. I did keep my empty blue jumbo one until I felt I could let it go for good.

While filling out the address to ship my stuff I had Tonia hovering over me like a schoolteacher—at least it felt like that. In her defense, the place was really small and very hot, and there was nowhere to go except maybe sitting on someone's lap! I had the pressure on me, a teacher standing beside me, and it felt like an SAT test. I crumbled and ended up spelling my name wrong! Who does that but me!?

MacGyver

For those who don't know who MacGyver is, MacGyver has an extraordinary knack for unconventional problem solving and an extensive bank of scientific knowledge that he believes can best be put to use to save lives.

There's always a little bit of MacGyver in all of us. From my skills of telling Jan how to fix the broken wheel on the overweight luggage with a butter knife, Shane trying to open up the safe with a 9V and tracking down his daughter's phone. But I must admit, Tonia is the true MacGyver. She has all of us beat with her bag of gadgets. No one on earth would think of bringing a clothesline with built-in clips and laundry detergent made out of paper for our stinky clothes. How wonderful it is to just have some clean underwear!

Okay, it's not like we are going through all of Europe with only our backpacks, but it is upsetting not to have the essentials in life. We just can't live without our hair straighteners, our sparkly shoes, and our lipsticks—I guess we'll make it with what we have. Oh, and Tonia had (legal) drugs for headaches, sleeping pills, indigestion, and allergies. You name it, she had it! I, on the other hand, brought some stupid items. Hair dye that doesn't have all the bottles of ingredients in the box to actually dye my hair, but do you think I would dare put the one

The clothes line

Nine Lives—Nine Purses

bottle in the trash? I bought it for ten dollars and have the other half at home. I was very lucky it didn't leak out on all my LVs! I had two sets of perfume with lip gloss on each end, *two for one how clever*, but why in the world did I end up bringing both sets? Maybe I don't have MacGyver traits after all?

Italy

Florence and The Hand Molester

Florence was the first stop in Italy. It's where I encountered the hand molester. He has the same name as Pinocchio's father, which is Geppetto. (I'm not kidding!) It felt like he was making out with my hand as he kissed it, not once, not twice – I honestly lost count. I believe there was tongue involved though!

Geppetto mentioned that he worked in the factory where the purses at the store were made. He was a wealth of information as well as being bored by himself. I instantly knew that Tonia and I were about to be educated on how purses were made and the correct way to hold them. We also knew we were going to be there for a while. I did glance outside the store to make sure our husbands were still around. They were very patient, I must say!

Geppetto took center stage, he wasn't going to leave anything out as he explained exactly how to hold a purse properly. He began by placing it on our forearms close to the elbow with your hand slightly in the air. He had to move my hand a couple of times into the right position. Then he told us when to use it as a crossbody and when to use it just over the shoulder. He was quite informative. He had mastered all the techniques and did everything with such conviction.

He informed us that we should never place a purse on the floor. It is a cardinal sin in the purse world! I watched him point his index finger in the air with a side-to-side motion as if saying no without actually saying the word out loud. Then he stopped and looked both of us in the eyes like a deer looking into headlights and said, "The only exception to being allowed to place your purse on the floor is when you give a signal to your friend that you are uncomfortable." We waited in anticipation for what to do when allowed to place your purse on the floor. He said, "By simply moving your purse from one side to another." This is a code that only eight percent of Italian women know about, but he wanted to pass this information on to us two American girls.

He then gave us a lesson on the differences between the Italian leathers and dyes and the Chinese street vendors that were selling theirs so cheaply.

He explained how his were made in a factory in Italy, not China. It takes twenty hours to complete one purse in his factory and he showed us the inside which was made with suede and also the thickness of the leather. The brilliant color of red is hand-rubbed! (Italians tend to use their hands a lot.)

The quality of the leather was far superior to any of the other purses that we saw but the best part was when he opened it up, it had a built-in light so things could be found in the dark. What an ingenious idea! Hook, line, and sinker, I found myself buying one. Was it a payment for him making out with my hand or was it a purse I really wanted or even needed?

You be the judge.

Innocence Lost

Also in Florence, innocence was taken from our sweet Mckinley. She had gotten a taste of how cruel this world can be. Two seconds changed her life, from enjoying her vacation, being with her family, coordinating our trip, texting her girlfriends, drinking her first alcoholic beverage, (not legal in the USA but legal in Europe) to sitting there with tears streaming down her face. All this because a grifter stole her phone and took her lifeline to her friends back home!

This beggar was very skilled at his profession and caught all six of us off guard! We had gone through France without being pick-pocketed in the crowded lines and streets—even in the sardine packed metros! We kept reminding each other to hold tight to our belongings. Just when we felt we were in somewhat of a safe place, sitting down eating and drinking together outside, with a white wood fence surrounding us, our purses in our laps, we became complacent. The one thing we thought would be okay sitting out were our phones. They were on the table just inches away from our hands. The beggar swiped it so quickly, and unexpectedly, that we didn't see it happening right under our noses! As I replay what had happened, over-and-over in my head, I believe instead of being a beggar he should be a magician.

He distracted us by waving his right hand up and down directly in front of our faces. While with his left hand he held a piece of paper that stated, "I need money." While he hid his hand underneath it, within two seconds, he grabbed the phone and left. We called the police, and they said they couldn't do anything and hung up.

I could see the hurt in McKinley's father's face as he wanted to jump into action like a superhero and pick the guy up by the throat for hurting his baby! Shane regrouped and did the next best thing by using what he does best and sprang into action with his phone.

Shane was tracking the movements of McKinley's phone on his. He wanted so badly to knock down the thief's door but knowing the consequences of confronting the assholl wasn't worth it. At first, it routed Shane back to the restaurant where we were eating to her watch on her wrist. At that moment is when we all started to laugh! Maybe we shouldn't mention that misdirecting part! (Not sure why I mentioned that part, but it was a little funny! We needed a little laughter after all the emotions of what just happened.)

Shane decided to track the phone on his iPad. Then he made the best decision to just let it go and turn off McKinley's phone altogether. Especially in a foreign country where the laws are so different than ours in the United States.

All the while, momma bear, Tonia, was still trying to track down the guy and if she had caught up with him, the story might have had a very different ending. Let's just say we would probably be visiting her in jail for manslaughter.

Tonia always looking at the silver lining in life says, "I believe this is a good thing to teach Mckinley. No matter how much you prepare for this not to happen, it still can."

Maybe it will open her eyes not to trust suspicious strangers anymore, but it still sucks!

Mckinley will be spending an extra month in Europe with some friends who live in England. I'll be talking about them when we get to England.

Reese has graciously allowed Mckinley to use her phone until it's replaced. Now, that's some sisterly love. Mckinley seems to be in better spirits and isn't letting this ruin her vacation. She did get some great news while here from the FBI, that they are considering her application!

Guess we know who will be on her most wanted list!

Wine Window

This loss didn't detour us from doing what we like to do best and that's drink. In Italy, it's legal to drink on the streets.

We went to what was called a wine window or *Buchetta deal Vino*, which was built over 400 years ago. It was made so they could cut out the middleman—a.k.a. the tax man. They were also used a lot during covid to limit contact during the pandemic.

Wine window in Italy

What's great about the whole experience is they serve the wine in a glass, not a paper cup. I want to mention the awesome place we stayed in while we were in Florence (despite the bad taste we all had in our mouths from what had happened to Mckinley). It was a memorable six-bedroom apartment with its breathtaking architecture and twenty-foot ceilings; it was like being in a castle with a ten-foot table. The kitchen had a balcony available to sit and enjoy meals.

Flintstones

I definitely can't forget the mammoth-size steaks! They were similar to the beginning of *The Flintstones* when Fred puts the steak on top of his car, and it leans sideways. You can also be the judge on what you think it looks like. *wink*

In the morning, when we were departing Florence, we had to catch an Uber at a central pick-up place. We began rolling the luggage

You be the judge

over some cobblestones. With each bump, it wasn't looking good for the pretty, pink, jumbo luggage. She hit one too many bumps and completely ripped her underbelly losing one of her wheels. She was a trooper, she barely held in there but now she was left with three legs. We knew sooner or later we would have to put her out of her misery and leave her jumbo size behind.

Rome

Rome was our next stop . . . again, the train ride was a nightmare, but we made it into Rome. Tonia and Shane had to do the walk of shame to the Fed Ex store because of their weight gain and now broken luggage. This is when the poor, pink, jumbo luggage girl was released to her final resting place; we had to part ways with her broken down self. Tonia and Shane became the new owners of our still holding-it-together blue, jumbo luggage.

"When in Rome,"(another thing I always wanted to say) we headed to Vatican City and the Sistine Chapel. We were dressed appropriately out of respect for the religious environment—a first for me! We ladies were

Final Resting Place

covered from our shoulders to our knees in the extreme heat of the July summer! I wanted to mention that July 2023 was one of the hottest months on record for Italy!

Dead Popes

Also, it may sound a little morbid, but Pope St. John XXIII was actually on display for the world to see in his resting place. To me, he looked like a wax figure, but it was his actual body! (Fact, the dead bodies of three Popes and a Russian saint are preserved and kept on display in the Basilica.) More surprisingly, though, there are 201 Popes buried beneath the church.

Cheese Wheel

One of the things Tonia wanted to do was try the cheese wheel. Parmesan cheese wheels take a whole year to age and 131 gallons of milk to make just one wheel. The average weight of a cheese wheel is about 88 pounds and can only be made in a restricted small area in Northern Italy called Parma, Italy.

It's impossible to make the exact same product outside of the production area. The reason why is that there are three good bacteria that only grow in that specific territory. Parmesan cheese is a big business for Italy. An average of 3.6 million wheels are produced each year.

Yumm

They begin by putting white wine inside the wheel and lighting it on fire, creating a cheese sauce. Then pasta is placed inside and spun around until the pasta gets coated with the cheese. Truffles are then added. Each of the cheese wheels can cost a restaurant $2,500 to $3,500!

Three Coin Toss

Trevi Fountain was a thing we had to experience; it carries the myth of the Three Coin Toss! It's said that if a person throws a coin into the fountain, a return to Rome is assured. A second coin launched promises a person will find love. The third coin is supposed to guarantee marriage. If you plan to throw a second and third coin into the fountain, each is to be tossed separately, not all at once. The proper way to toss a coin is to use your right hand to throw the coin over your left shoulder. The money is donated to Rome's Catholic Charity, Caritas, which funds soup kitchens, homeless shelters, and other projects. Approximately 1.4 million euros are thrown into the fountain each year.

Lock and Key

The Colosseum was on the agenda for the next day. A cute, little Italian woman with a thick accent was our guide. I had promised the Covered Bridge staff, family, and friends that I would place their locks and keys I had carried with me in my backpack on the fence in Paris, France. Jan and I placed ours there ten years previously. But the fence happened to have fallen over from the heavy weight.

Unloading the steel

Since the fence wasn't replaced, I decided the next best place would be in Rome, a great religious place. I was glad to unload them because the locks were so heavy!

Tonia and I paid a hefty price for sneaking off from our group to accomplish our mission of placing the locks and keys on the fence. The 4-foot 8-inch, not-so-sweet, Italian woman gave us a stern look upon our return. Remember, Tonia was in cahoots with me, so even a teacher can get into trouble with another teacher!

Naples

Naples was memorable with the airbnb. It was definitely a diamond in the rough. On the outside and the surrounding area, you would think you were in Harlem, with all the graffiti on the sides of the building. We all looked at each other in disbelief. Could there be a mistake in the choice of where we would be staying? However, we were led up the stairs to what looked like an oasis, to a suite that was tastefully and beautifully remodeled. The manager there was a sweet girl who translated for the owner and reassured us it was very safe; she was right.

Ginormous door

Holding Down a Job While Gripping Louie

There's just way too much to see and so little time to enjoy the beauty of what's on this earth. It's hard to wrap my head around the fact that the places we visited during our trip have been here in all their beauty for over 2000 years; from the gladiator fights to today's common people just making a living by making pizza, spaghetti, or bread.

Too sexy

Best Pizza Ever!

We ate so much pizza that we couldn't eat any more for the rest of our visit. We came to a mutual agreement that the very best pizza we ate, while in Italy, was in Naples at a place called The L'Antica pizzeria Da Michele, which has been in existence since 1890. It reminded us of a pizzeria in New York city, but there are differences: the price of a pizza was only €5.50, which is unheard of in this day and age. The Italian workers were extremely nice, so nice they didn't mind stopping and taking pictures with a little half-Japanese girl who snuck in (uninvited) and headed towards the back to get a picture with chefs.

The street was so crowded with people waiting patiently, there was no arguing, no fighting, and no cutting in line. It seemed that people wanted to taste the pizza so badly that they were willing to wait their turn. The lines never ended; the people just kept

Nine Lives—Nine Purses

coming. They can put out 90 pizzas an hour using a wood oven stove. The pizza was so delicious that it was in the movie that Julia Roberts starred in, *Eat, Pray, Love*. If you watch it, you will actually see them filming her at a table inside the very tiny pizzeria.

We waited for well over an hour in the hot sun to find out for ourselves what all the hype was about. We decided on the Margherita pizza. It's hard to explain in words the taste, the texture, the crust, the tomato sauce, the basil, and the best cheese that you can only get from this region. It was so good that we didn't mind that we were eating with a view of trash cans ten feet away from us. We sat down on the only place we could find, the curb on the street with very little shade, but no one

Uninvited Jap

Pizza nirvana

42

complained. We all just sat and enjoyed each bite as well as each other's company in the hot sticky sun knowing the temperature was well over a hundred degrees!

Pizza School

The pizza school was a blast! It was well worth attending and probably taught Jan a thing or two. All of us got to mix the dough, form it into a roundish shape, at least we tried, and then place the different ingredients on it.

The important part was the delicious cheese, which made a big difference in the taste; once again we agreed the Da Michele pizza was top notch! We were told how to correctly eat a pizza is to fold the tip up and then fold the crust in half and start eating. We looked at each other thinking we misunderstood and being the foreigners that we were in their country, we picked it up in single slices. When we went back to our hotel to Google the correct way of eating a pizza. In Italy, they fold it twice and then begin eating!

The gang

Disappointment

I had gotten such a rush from my experience with Louie Vuitton that I wanted to check out another luxury designer while in Italy and that's Gucci. So, I asked the gang if they would mind stopping there for me. Unselfishly, they all were up for it, but we weren't greeted with a warm welcome like the Louie Vuitton store. The sales lady was very disappointing, to say the least, she had no personality. We were in and out quickly. I had to get my cat eye sunglasses that reminded me of my trip to Paris and *Breakfast at Tiffany's*, plus getting my first designer footwear, some slides (sandals) that Brooke told me that I must have because my old crocs needed a resting place — in the trash!

The following day we were off to the Amalfi Coast. It was exhausting because of the extreme heat, it was well over 100 degrees, and I couldn't get cool at all. They had A/C in the van, but it was just hot air blowing around. We began driving up high in the mountains by the windy cliff edge and the driver kept hitting the brakes. We were supposed to go on a boat ride, but I had gotten car sick and knew I couldn't handle a boat ride now.

The boys

Our tour guide was a very interesting Italian woman who shared with us that she had spent the night before at a concert, so she had little sleep, but she did a great job of explaining things to us in three different languages. It was amazing to hear her speak English, Italian, and Spanish without skipping a beat!

Lessons from a pro

Holding Down a Job While Gripping Louie

Next, we were taken to tour the Pompeii ruins and had a very passionate, young, Italian man who really knew his history and didn't want to leave anything out on his two-hour tour in the heat of the afternoon. He was funny because he didn't like them restoring the original walls, which if they didn't it would have eventually crumbed. He just kept pointing out the modern versus the original.

Venice

Venice was probably one of our favorite spots in Italy and it was definitely the cleanest.

I want to go on record about being a certified WSSI because we have to take a boat to our hotel on an island. If the boat goes down, I will ONLY be saving my Louie's! Everyone else will have to fend for themselves.

As soon as we got off the plane, we had to catch a boat to our hotel. It's hard to imagine having to get from island to island by boat and seeing every building surrounded by water up to their front doors, where you literally have to step onto a platform. One step can determine if you are on dry land or drenched in sea water!

Tom Cruise

We, of course, had to see what Venice was all

Wide Eyes Shut

45

Nine Lives—Nine Purses

about, and not doing my due diligence beforehand, (except with purses) I just winged it, like how I get through life. Thank God, Tonia had all the knowledge of what to expect.

While venturing out we decided it was important to do some laundry. That task should have taken us fifteen minutes to walk to the laundry but ended up taking 2-1/2 hours. We kind of got sidetracked by a shop display of beautiful masks. We had to go inside, especially when we found that the shop was famous for the masks that were created for the movie *Eyes Wide Shut* starring Tom Cruise.

Jan told me he would buy one for me, seven masks later . . . that's how hard it was to pick out just one mask! Plus, it's like potato chips, you can't just have one.

We finally found our way to the laundry mat.

The glass blowing factory

Miami Or Bust!

Next, it was time to visit the Murano glass factory. I'll be honest and state that I never really paid much attention to glass blowing and the designs that are created. That was until we met the little, old, Italian guy who was retired and volunteered his time, to show us how to blow glass. Why did he

Holding Down a Job While Gripping Louie

volunteer? Because he needed time away from his wife who was driving him crazy! He wanted to know where we were from and I answered, "Florida."

He became so excited and just kept saying, "Miami," over and over with the biggest smile on his face.

Tonia and I looked at each other and nodded our heads in agreement and said, "Yes, Miami!"

He then said, "I love Miami!"

Who wants to crush a little, old, Italian man's image of people flying in to see him from Miami?!

We found a restaurant that we loved so much that we had three of our meals there and by the end of it, they treated us like family. So much so, that we were given free shots of alcohol each time! Most importantly, we went there not just for the tasty food but for the air conditioning!

Venice is also known for the James Bond movies of which several have been filmed there. The wooden speed boats that were used are still there.

Gondola

Lastly, we had to experience a Gondola ride! It was breathtaking with the romantic, slow ride, while the man rowing

Gondolier

47

stood behind us, in his striped shirt doing all the work with the precision of a watchmaker making turns in very tight spaces. It was amazing, to say the least. We found out that to become a gondolier is a family vocation, it is passed down to the family from father to son. Not a bad living when it's about $120 for 30 minutes for four people.

Thinking back on our experiences of being in France and Italy, the air conditioning really played a big part of how different America can be from Europe. In most parts of America to walk out of a restaurant, department store, or even a person's home that didn't have A/C, it's just unheard of! We have been so spoiled. People in Florida have died from heat exhaustion, especially if they aren't used to the heat and don't hydrate properly. We found out very quickly that the air conditioning in Europe is not a neccessity. Ninety percent of places don't have A/C and if they do, they conserve the hell out of it! An example is one in Naples, the airbnb that we stayed at, they wanted to conserve so much that as soon as you opened the terrace door to walk out and have a cup of coffee the A/C would automatically shut off. My question is, doesn't it take more energy to get the A/C up and running again to cool off the place?

England

We were jetting off once again, (I've always wanted to say that too) to the beautiful countryside of Manchester, England!

We were staying with a lovely English family. That was far better than the airbnb we stayed in. The hosts adopted us into their family circle. The first day we had a traditional English brunch that consisted of pork and beans on buttered toast with brown sauce (Daddies sauce) with 22 people, most of them were Lynn and Phillip's kids and grandkids.

I really want to tell you about the charming personalities of our hosts. Lynn is a proper English lady who belongs to a golf club and puts so much of her energy into it, that it's almost like her baby. It keeps her busy and, by the sound of it, the ladies really appreciate the many hours that she contributes. We have developed a common interest in our designer bags. She wanted to see my stash of Louie's.

I told her I didn't mind bringing out the ladies (that's what I call them) for a breather. It was like I was introducing them, and they were the stars of the evening. But before I could even take them out of their dust protection pouches, Lynn reminded me to wash my hands to remove any oils that might be on my hands. (I have to ask myself if it's worth all the responsibilities of caring for these exquisite beauties? Overwhelmingly, the answer was hell yeah!)

One-by-one they made their appearance. It was almost like marching soldiers in all their glory, and I was their proud owner! I did wait for the grand finale, to bring out my most valuable and favorite one, the one I did so much research on; to me she is the queen of England. We all waited in anticipation as I gingerly pulled Miss Capucine's dust cover clothes off her leather body to be displayed; she didn't disappoint!

Phillip, Lynn's husband is a character, he has a funny wit, he is a speed talker. Always speaking so quickly and then laughing. It's almost like he talks in a question form; so nodding your head in agreement isn't always the way to go, even if you can understand him. I found myself having to listen carefully. Jan has his, "I can't hear very well," so everyone gives him a pass for not always understanding.

Ladies And Gentlemen, The Beatles

Lynn and Phillip graciously took us to Liverpool, England for the day and we went to where the Beatles were from and played when they began their careers in a bar called The Cavern. We were in awe knowing that they got their start there.

Lamb's Inn

Afterwards, we had to have another traditional English meal that is well-known—fish and chips with a side of mushy peas. When you're hungry, the mushy peas are worth at least trying.

The following night we weren't disappointed with going to a favorite place that Lynn and Phillip recommended and that was, The Lambs Inn. I, of course, couldn't eat a cute baby lamb, but everyone said it was delicious. My meal consisted of tender beef with brown gravy and Yorkshire pudding with cauliflower and cheese. I must say it was quite tasty, especially for England, which isn't known for tasty food. At least that's what I hear.

Road Rage?

We had rented a car; Shane was the driver, which I must say isn't an easy task. We arrived in the wee hours of the morning, about 1:00 a.m., so the visibility wasn't the best. On top of everything else, Englanders drive on the opposite side of the road, so that's a double whammy! Shane did extremely well, but I can't say much for the mirrors, bushes, scraping trees, cutting off cars, and driving straight through a roundabout! Hey, that's what insurance is for! Joking aside, he did great! I didn't see any of the rest of us volunteering for the job.

I want to mention what brought us and our English family together. His name was Brian, Lynn's father. Brian passed in 2022 but I must say he did live life to the fullest! We love and miss you, Brian, very much!

Aishitemasu Brian San!

Now, it was time for us to say our goodbyes to our English family and the kindness they showed us! We had to catch a train for the last leg of our European Vacation. We were off to London.

London

We arrived in London and didn't want to waste any time, so off we went to tour the London Eye. Tonia made sure we got the VIP treatment with complimentary champagne. What a gal!

Then it was on to the Tower of London where it has displayed the Crown Jewels since 1661. It has a long tradition of storing precious objects there. It's so over the top and beautiful to look at behind all the glass and steel security. Also, with its magnificent world-famous collection of 23,578 gemstones, it is part of the Royal Collection and boasts items that are still used in royal ceremonies today.

A toast to good times.

Tower of London

McDonald's

We went to McDonald's last night just to check it out because Jan and I went to it ten years ago, but they have since closed in the area. However, we remembered another and went to the train station, not too far away.

They serve chicken wraps which have been discontinued in the states. They also served mozzarella balls and curry sauce! The sodas have no ice! We looked around for a garbage can and there was none to be found. We asked the manager to let us use the one behind the counter and he told us they aren't allowed to have them in the restaurant for the public to use.

A taste of home

(Because of safety purposes) Stupid me said, "What if we had a bomb in our trash and you let us use yours?!" He smiled at me, and I told myself maybe that wasn't a good thing to say.

Harrods

We had to visit Harrods. It's a very expensive place with all the Luxury Designers stores one right after the other under one roof. It's the second most visited area besides the Palace in England.

Nine Lives—Nine Purses

All I purchased was a tea tin with the queen's picture on it that plays music, it cost only L13 and I got a nice shopping bag with the name Harrods on it.

There was a mini-Harrods at the London airport so . . . shopping again for last-minute goodies was on my agenda!

First Class!

My man got us first-class seats coming back home. We are like hicks, we don't know how to act, so we are sitting here with drinks, along with the unlimited wine which Jan took advantage of, and we haven't even taken off! I believe he has a little fear of flying so a little apple juice helped calm his nerves.

We have our own TV right in front of us; there's so much leg room that I stood up and did my happy dance. Also, the seats reclined. Of course, we were offered a pillow with a matching blanket for a little shuteye. No more flying like common people, we felt like royalty. We were like the Jeffersons, "We were moving on up!" What a difference from how we had come to Europe on our flight over, sitting in coach.

Thank God, Jan paid for them because you know I'm too cheap to spend money on first class! If they had given me a discount, I would have helped fly the plane by flapping my arms.

Dreading Customs

We landed and the fun was about to start—going through customs! I had watched videos of what to expect while going through customs. All the YouTube videos said not to fib about how much I spent.

With technology today, Customs knows how to track your purchases. They would know exactly how much a person had spent from their VAT refund filing. This is the European refund tax that only foreigners are allowed to claim. They can also track it with the use of a passport.

So, I was completely ready for the uniformed Customs guy with his spotlight shining in my eyes and the interrogation of the "what's and why's" of what I had brought back with me in my luggage. With the sweat rolling down my face, I just knew how one slip of the tongue could land me in the slammer.

They wanted to know if you were brave or stupid enough to bring back a white powdery substance but all I had were the Louie Vuittons. (They were more important to me!) I knew the canine dogs would be ready and able to sniff whatever I had and that was the Corinthian leather of my Louie's.

Beat The System

I was prepared; I had done all my research on what to expect, and it was time to do the walk-through customs. I followed the signs and kept going and looking and found that I had walked past everything. How on earth with all the Homeland Security could I dodge it? There just happened to be a cop and so I approached with a little panic and also guilt on my face asking him where in the world Customs was and he told me I already went through it and directed me to continue moving along. Did I click my heels and imagine it was all just a dream? Did I beat the system and wouldn't have to declare what I had purchased and not have to pay Uncle Sam for allowing me to spend all my hard-earned money? Or would I get into trouble eventually? Would I be going to the Slammer? Maybe I shouldn't admit I didn't go through Customs altogether!

Kiss And Tell

Tonia and her family, minus Mckinley, who was staying in England an extra month, had taken a different route back and landed in Orlando which went without a hiccup.

So of course, I had to call Tonia and ask her if she had gone through Customs with her Louie Vuittons and she did and said it went smoothly. Her advice to me was, "Oh well, just keep going!"

I have always believed in the saying, "It's better to beg for forgiveness than to ask for permission." It's a way of life. It's not about abusing the situation but about knowing when to push the boundaries. It's like having an angel on one shoulder and a devil on the other.

So, I would have to bookmark it for another day. We had to keep moving because we had to make a connecting flight to another airport.

It's A Wonderful Life

This is when you might say to yourself, "What a wonderful way to end the flight back from a 3-1/2 week, once-in-a-lifetime vacation." It wasn't over yet!

We were brought down a notch with our first-class upgrade flight because we were delayed for eight hours. Back to coach class we went, sitting with our knees to our chest!

Home Sweet Home!

We finally arrived in Tampa, Florida with a sigh of relief and a bag of expensive purses from Paris, which by then I had carried for well over 3-1/2 weeks in and out of planes, trains, cars, taxis, buses, and boats. I realized my dream of being the proud owner of all my Louie's. It was 4:00 a.m. and I had to work the next day, so I quickly fell asleep in my own bed. It felt great!

This is when I'm supposed to end my story of my European Vacation and as Dorothy said, in the Wizard of Oz movie, "There's no place like home!"

If you have read to this point, you're obviously interested in what I had to say, or you're overly bored, but for whatever reason I do appreciate it.

Back To The Grind

I woke up and began my regular life schedule of getting ready for work at the Covered Bridge. I sipped my coffee while watching YouTube until the very last moment when I had to get into my car. I race down the road because I'm late, again! I talked on the phone with Maria, my best friend, about what I'm doing with my life and turning the corner on two wheels while driving into the parking lot. Not much has changed at the Covered Bridge or so I thought.

Goodbye Is Hard

Not one person at the Covered Bridge wanted to spoil my vacation with bad news. It was Joyce, the Matriarch of the family, the wife, the mother, the sister, and our boss. Joyce made working at the Covered Bridge enjoyable with her quick wit. She always seemed to joke around with everyone! She would sit at the breakfast bar with her legs folded into a pretzel for hours at a time playing Candy Crush on her phone. She would always tell each of us how much she loved us in her sweet voice. Joyce joined the angels in heaven after I came back from Europe. I got to say my goodbyes. She will always have a special place in my heart.

Aishitemasu Joyce San!

The Final Curtain

Before I end this non-stop rambling and close the curtains on the adventure of a lifetime, I wanted to put in this book that I purchased an amazing 8-foot-tall cabinet that houses all my new Louie Vuittons so that they are protected from all the elements that can make them less than perfect. I have them proudly displayed in my bedroom 7-1/2 feet from me so I can say good night to them each night!

Stone Pizza Oven

My husband had ordered a commercial size stone pizza oven, eight months before we even made the trip, and it arrived shortly after our return! (Great timing on his part.)

Nine Lives—Nine Purses

Protecting my Louies

Stone pizza oven

Now, we will definitely need to make pizzas for profit to pay for the pizza oven, the trip, the Louie Vuittons, our retirement, and to keep both of us from being greeters at Walmart once we are into our retirement!

Was putting my life history of everything that had happened to me, gripping Luxury Louies for the 3-1/2 weeks in a backpack, and the wonderful trip all worth it? I wouldn't have changed a thing!

The End . . . for now

About the Author

SHEILA SCHULTZ grew up in a military family and consequently traveled considerablly. As a child she lived in Lubbock, Texas. In her high school years she had to switch countries and travel to the Far East, to Japan which is the home of her mother's family.

Sheila graduated high school while living on the beautiful Island of Okinawa, Japan. After graduation she was discovered at a Shakey's Pizza Parlor and became a model in Tokyo. Finallly, she set her roots in the quaint little town of Dunedin, Florida where she married and raised two children.

Sheila has gone through so many challenges with her jobs from being a model in Tokyo to being a hospice caregiver for animals! She has tried to look at life as a journey, and an adventure, and is willing to take the lead on whatever she puts her mind to. She believes there is no such thing as failure, but just a stepping stone to accomplishing what she puts her mind to.

Sheila wrote this book with the hope that her granddaughters will get an understanding and appreciation of their Sheshe and what she has experienced in her life.

She hopes that when her granddaughters are ready to conquer the world, they will take chances and never be afraid of change just like their Sheshe!

Made in the USA
Columbia, SC
09 December 2024

be06824c-8576-46a8-a136-7418dc601e82R01